THE BEST OF
ERIC TREACY

THE BEST OF
ERIC TREACY

LONDON NEW YORK SYDNEY TORONTO

Frontispiece

Queen Mary *on Shap. Undoubtedly one of Treacy's most famous photographs. Stanier Pacific No 6222 is in perfect order, running with a 'clear chimney', as she effortlessly romps up Shap with the Coronation Scot for Glasgow in the summer of 1939. What a glorious sound she must have been making climbing the bank at around sixty miles per hour.*

Jacket photographs

Front *Edge Hill cutting was one of Eric Treacy's favourite locations. The sun was only high enough during the six weeks of mid-summer and then only for about an hour or so, during which time the 10.00* Merseyside Express *climbed out of Liverpool, Lime Street for London, Euston. On this morning in the early 1950s the express was hauled by rebuilt Patriot class No 45525* Colwyn Bay. *These locomotives were a firm favourite with crews who found them more economical and better riding than the more usual rebuilt Royal Scots employed on this duty.*

Back *The west end of Leeds City station was a hive of activity regularly captured on film by Treacy. Here the LMS and LNER departed side by side. On this occasion during 1950, Class 5 No 45424 waits impatiently for departure whilst D49 Hunt class 4–4–0 No 62738* The Zetland *is surrounded by steam from the injector overflow pipe, as it double heads a train out of the station. A real atmospheric scene wonderfully captured.*

Acknowledgments

No one knows the Treacy negatives better than John Smart who spent his introduction to publishing working on the catalogue of the 10,000 images. Aided by John Edgington and David Johnson, the best of the best was sorted to form the final selection. Prints were made from the negatives by June Lawrence to whom we owe special thanks. The introduction was provided by David St John Thomas and for the concept of the book itself we wish to record our indebtedness to the late Patrick Whitehouse whose foresight has placed the Treacy collection in its rightful place in the records of British railway photography.

First published by
David St John Thomas Publisher
an imprint of Thomas & Lochar

This edition published 1994
by BCA by arrangement with Thomas & Lochar

CN 5908

© David St John Thomas (Introduction) and Millbrook House Ltd 1994

Book designed by Michael Head
Typeset by XL Publishing Services, Nairn
Printed in Great Britain by Butler & Tanner, Frome

CONTENTS

INTRODUCTION

That collections of any photographer's work should be published steadily over a period of half a century is remarkable enough; that they should be railway photographs by a cleric who rose to the rank of bishop is one of those quirks that characterise the history of the arts. And art is definitely what we are talking about in the work of Eric Treacy. As he put it: 'I am wanting to do with my camera what I could only do with a box of water colours... to catch that indefinable spell of railways, to make visual something that can only be felt.'

During my adolescence, I would bring an occasional letter from Treacy to my father along with the rest of his post. The effect was magic. I, too, had come under that 'indefinable spell', sometimes to be teased about it (especially by female relations) as though it were a rather conspicuous physical defect. Not only was Treacy's work extremely appealing in itself, but its very existence seemed to acknowledge that the love of railways was permissible. That thousands almost worshipped his work seemed to give licence for lesser mortals to experience the awe of an express train mounting a scenic summit or thundering out of a tunnel.

Many of my generation must have felt Treacy's influence and been encouraged in their individual artistic appreciation of our railways. There were, indeed, many such even among ministers of religion. Though Treacy set the standard that many who took their own pictures aspired to, it of course involved a great deal more than just photography... the aesthetic

Edge Hill cutting was surely the most remarkable of Treacy's locations. It was only available for a few days of the year when the sun was at its zenith and bright enough to penetrate into the gloomy depths. Careful planning of late morning visits produced some of his own favourite pictures, such as this view of unrebuilt Royal Scot No 6130 The West Yorkshire Regiment *leaving Liverpool for Euston with the 11.15am up express in 1939.*

desire to capture and experience an entire unique way of life.

Indefinable it has always been, but we know (and Treacy sometimes quoted) some of its elements. It was the working railway that employed a unique, committed labour force usually employed well away from the rest of mankind while serving the nation – sons often treading in their father's and grandfather's shoes. The figure standing on the track in the jacket photograph of this book perhaps sums it up best, although often Treacy caught the locomotive men at their work and knew some intimately, indeed acknowledging them in some of the captions of his earlier books.

The locomotive itself was however the principal actor. Making its own power as it went on its way (indeed sometimes using more power than currently being made), it knit the nation together carrying people and goods around it. It also represented Britain's industrial gift to the world. And in its widely different forms it reflected Britain's different regional, historical, cultural and mechanical backgrounds. Shap would have been quite different had it been served by a railway of different lineage. Locomotives of different antiquity in different liveries reflected the mood almost as much as the terrain and weather.

The backgrounds were vital, and one of the joys of Treacy's work is that he became intimate with a select but diverse range of locations in their changing moods. They were like theatrical sets on which the action took place. Yet understanding the total railway, how it all dovetailed together, how for example one locomotive crew's heroic efforts could help traffic miles away, was also important if you were to tell the whole story. To take one example, if they or their captions do not actually reveal it, the excitement of the best shots of the Settle & Carlisle is heightened by the knowledge that nothing has stirred hereabouts for some time past: you can *feel* the contrast between the long silences and the total attention the train

In the old Euston. The Pastor to railwaymen stands with the driver of Royal Scot class No 6109 Royal Engineer *before a footplate journey to his home town of Liverpool.*

demanded when it eventually passed. *Patterns* of activity were something that Treacy often commented on in his own introductions... waxing eloquent, for example, about the way a seemingly deserted country station came back to life with the arrival of a few passengers and the signalman and how drama then took place at the platforms when a train or two halted to do their business, perhaps including the taking of water by the tank engines.

It is perhaps not surprising that ultimately the steam railway has attracted its own school of painters, people who have used an actual box of water colours (or oils) and had the advantage of being able to create their own compositions by moving things around a

bit to suit artistic convenience and better portray the magic. I like to think that Treacy was the first in their line! Unlike most of them who have had to recreate period images, he was around recording history as it happened… the most important of a small group who however did a great deal more than *just* record.

In one of his letters to my father, I recall Treacy indeed emphasising that he was not interested in taking as many pictures or even recording as many different types of locomotives and trains at different locations as possible because he wanted to 'get the magic'. The problem, he admitted, was that some people did not or could not appreciate that… and he was everlastingly being asked what kind of camera he used. That was as irrelevant as asking a writer what kind of pen or typewriter he employed as though the quality of the writing depended on the technical equipment.

Provided it was adequate, he kept telling those interested in his work, the choice of camera was far less important than the way in which it was used. To be sure, it had to be mastered technically, but only as a means to an end. Likewise, you had to realise technical limitations. A perfectionist, Treacy thus hardly ever (and never until faster films became available after the war) took pictures other than in sunshine, and then avoided too bright conditions which would prevent the steam locomotive's exhaust showing up. Good shots also depended on adequate homework, noting what position the sun would be in when the

Southern Pacific No 35019 French Line CGT, *attached to an LMS tender to provide a water scoop facility, heads out from Leeds with the 7.50am to King's Cross on one of the trial trips run in advance of the official tests during the Locomotive Exchanges of 1948. A favourite vantage point was Beeston Junction, south of Leeds with its characteristic Great Northern Railway somersault signalling.*

chosen train was due, how something in the foreground might emphasise the size of the locomotive, and so on. It also frequently involved requesting enginemen artificially to boost the exhaust at the critical moment. Drivers and firemen in his congregation helped him become familiar with depots and more crews… and led to his entry in *Who's Who* giving 'pottering around locomotive depots' as his pastime.

Treacy was probably never happier than when in the company of working railwaymen, and increasingly worked with them in partnership, ensuring they had a print of appropriate photographs… and being disappointed as much on their behalf as his own if an exposure went wrong. Often the partnership helped make the best of his limited opportunities, time and money preventing the lengthy expeditions that enthusiasts of more recent times have come to take for granted. He indeed took up photography in the first place (before being captured by the magic of railways) seeking a hobby that would not be too time-demanding knowing that being a parson would give him relatively little leisure time. Often he was restricted to quarter an hour morning and evening.

It is details like this, emphasising that in some ways Treacy was a very ordinary man, that make his achievement the more remarkable. Born in 1907, in 1932 he became deacon of the Church of England at Liverpool, marrying in the same year. While at Liverpool he ran a large boys' club and first became interested in photography, and soon bought his first serious camera, a small 35mm Leica. Between 1936 and 1940, he was vicar of Edge Hill, Liverpool. Already his work was familiar to readers of the *Railway Magazine*. In 1935 he had joined the Railway Photographic Society under Maurice Earley.

By the late 1930s his style had become instantly recognisable, the emphasis being on trains well-lit by the sun moving slowly so he could capture them

The BR Britannia class Pacifics made the Great Eastern a new railway for a time in the 1950s. They were master of their task, well looked after and a reputed favourite with the crews. During 1954 No 70001 Lord Hurcomb *waits for the right away with the Norfolkman express, whilst No 70002* Geoffrey Chaucer *enters Liverpool Street station with the Hook Continental boat train from Harwich.*

Left *An all too brief glimpse of sunlight flashes over the wet sleepers as the final Princess Coronation built, No 46257* City of Salford, *approaches Thrimby Grange with an up express in appalling weather conditions. Footplate journeys were a special privilege not granted to many. Treacy has recorded the driver's side view, approaching the LNWR pattern home signal.*

more sharply. Especially well remembered are the action shots of trains ascending Shap and leaving Liverpool. Between 1937 and 1939 he took holidays in the Lake District partly because of its proximity to Shap.

In 1940 he volunteered and became chaplain to the forces, perhaps taking possibly his best Shap picture in 1942 when on leave in the Lake District. He was awarded the MBE for work in the forces, which he left in 1945 when he was appointed Rector of Keighley, the Midland's Aire Valley route being only a few miles away. The next year, 1946, saw publication of his first book or rather booklet, the first title in the LMS series of *My Best Railway Photographs* published by Ian Allan at 1s 6d.

His pictures were now appearing in *Trains Illustrated* as well as the *Railway Magazine*. More booklets were published, and in 1949 came his first major work, *Steam Up*, in which he emphasised that his approach 'is emotional rather than technical', again talked about capturing the spirit of the total railway and its aesthetic beauty and criticised ultra-purist experts. He was the person who went to the concert hall to enjoy the total experience, not to be told the evening had been ruined by some inaccuracy in the score! He went on to produce another eight books in his lifetime.

The 1949 locomotive exchanges gave him a special challenge. Clerical duties limited his range and opportunities but he captured some remarkable scenes. The

Opposite *A Treacy scoop. Class A1 4–6–2 No 60161* North British *brings the three-cylinder LNER sound to Shap at the head of the 11.15am Birmingham to Glasgow express. Between 1951 and 1953 Nos 60152/60/1 were allocated to the former LMS shed at Polmadie in Glasgow to work west coast route trains on a trial basis.*

same year he became Archdeacon of Halifax and later Suffrage Bishop of Pontefract, which he remained until 1961, (and took the position again between 1968 and 1976) along with that of Bishop of Wakefield. He is of course best known as Bishop of Wakefield, and many of we lesser mortals in the world of railway enthusiasm noted with glee that his pottering around locomotive sheds had prevented the fulfilment of his career.

He retired in 1976, to Keswick. The following year he was nominated by the Secretary of State to sit on the council of the Friends of the National Railway Museum, and involvement with the railway preservation movement included his becoming president of the Keighley and Worth Valley Preservation Society as well as that of the Tyseley Railway Museum in Birmingham.

After steam ceased on BR in August 1968, he did photograph diesels, and remarked that if you had to have such uninteresting things then at least the Deltics were the best of the bunch. He also experimented with colour, but his colour work never towered above that of other people's as his black and white did.

He died on 13 May 1978 while photographing a special train hauled appropriately by *Evening Star*, at one of his favourite retirement locations, Appleby Station, where there is a memorial to him. In May the following year his widow unveiled the name of a new electric locomotive, *Bishop Treacy*.

Having been under his spell during my formative years and well beyond, it was then my great pleasure to publish a number of posthumous works, working with Patrick Whitehouse who had known him well and cherished the collection of his negatives, especially the glass plates of pre-war days. Happily, improvements in scanning and printing technology meant that quality became steadily better and perhaps for the first time the full magic of Treacy could be savoured in print.

For a long time Patrick Whitehouse and I had discussed an ultimate tribute to Treacy, a high-quality landscape book to go along with latter-day collections of railway paintings. The last letter I received from Patrick before his sudden death in June 1993 implored me to write this introduction. There is in truth little new I or anyone else could say, for the pictures speak for themselves. Just one point: do as it were to stand back from them and see them as pictures, not a record of nuts and bolts... and experience the thrill of being there. This book, then, is offered in homage to the memories of the artist of railway photographers and to my co-author of ten books whose love of the photographs made this volume possible.

DAVID ST JOHN THOMAS

The prototype Deltic diesel with its arresting livery immediately captured Treacy's attention. This superb 1957 view shows it passing Edge Hill with the up Merseyside Express whilst undergoing trials on the London Midland Region. However, the 22 production examples, built from 1961, all ran on the east coast route out of King's Cross. Although first and foremost a steam photographer Treacy did record the transitional period of the 1960s in some detail and the Deltics became his most popular diesel subject.

Around the time of nationalisation the old companies were just beginning to explore the alternatives to steam traction. Ivatt on the LMS produced the first main line diesel-electric locomotive No 10000 during 1947, in collaboration with English Electric. This was followed in 1948 by a second No 10001. The locomotives were only rated at 1600hp, so on the heavier main line duties they worked together. The pair are seen here leaving Preston with an up express in 1948.

LIVERPOOL

▶ *The thunderous exhaust of Jubilee class No 45681 Aboukir raises the echoes as the LMS 4–6–0 gets under way from Liverpool Lime Street and heads into the sulphurous cutting. The picture was taken in the first years of nationalisation when liveries, for both locomotives and rolling stock, were in a state of flux.*

◀ *This photograph was taken in the early 1950s when British Railways' first livery styles had become settled. In this instance Brunswick green for the locomotive and red and cream for the coaches. Jubilee class 4–6–0 No 45596 Bahamas heads an express out of the city, at Edge Hill, in the early 1950s. No 45596 is now preserved, although not in this guise, as it subsequently received a double chimney and larger tender.*

◀ *A third Jubilee No 45600 Bermuda stands at the buffer stops of Lime Street with a local train from Manchester. Treacy observed the magical effects of light and shade and steam on a visit to Lime Street in the early 1930s. It was perhaps a platform end view similar to this that gave him the inspiration to try railway photography.*

▲ *Edge Hill No 2, a typical LNWR pattern box, can be seen on the left as class 2P 4–4–0 No 471 pilots Patriot No 5527 Southport out of Liverpool with a southbound express in the late 1930s. The large number of sheeted wagons shows just how much freight was carried in open vehicles throughout the steam era.*

▶ *Another view taken from the steps of Edge Hill No 2 signal box finds LMS class 5 4–6–0 No 5148, in post-war guise, hauling an express of non-corridor stock. The photograph is full of railway atmosphere, from the LNWR pattern signals to the bewildering variety of wagons on show.*

▲ *Two Royal Scot class 4–6–0s are caught side by side. On the left No 6155* The Lancer *takes the three coach Liverpool portion of the Sunny South Express to Crewe. Whilst on the right No 6112* Sherwood Forester *is probably waiting to set back into Lime Street. On the Picton Road overbridge a Liverpool streamlined tram heads towards Wavertree Road.*

◀ *Edge Hill station can still be seen in the background of this photograph under the bridge. The junction signal above the first and second coaches shows that Camden based Princess Royal class Pacific No 6208* Princess Helena Victoria *is returning south with the up Merseyside Express in the late 1930s.*

▶ *The fireman leans out of the cab of Princess Coronation class Pacific No 6232* Duchess of Montrose *to confirm his pre-arranged exhaust effects are appreciated by the photographer. The locomotive is passing Edge Hill goods depot with the up Merseyside Express in 1938/9.*

This group of late 1930s and 40s pictures shows ex-LNWR express engines hard at work in the Liverpool area. Still a reasonably common part of the scene before the war, when Treacy returned to photograph in Merseyside afterwards they had virtually disappeared.

▶ A Chester based Precursor class 4–4–0 No 25188 Marquis rounds the curve towards Wavertree Junction with a parcels train in the late 1930s. On the right the coaling stage of Edge Hill shed is partly obscured by a coal stack.

◀ The last Claughton 4–6–0 No 6004 (formerly named Princess Louise) heads a fitted freight at Edge Hill in the immediate post-war era. The locomotive was finally withdrawn, from Edge Hill shed, in April 1949.

◀ George the Fifth class 4–4–0 No 25376 Snipe passes Wavertree Junction box with a down local train around 1937. A clerestory corridor third, of Midland Railway design, heads a non-corridor formation.

◀ *The unique LMS 'Turbomotive' steam turbine driven 4–6–2 No 6202, now fitted with smoke deflectors, passes Wavertree with the 5.25pm Liverpool-London express c 1939. This was a regular working for the locomotive both before and after the war. When the turbines required replacing in the early 1950s it was decided to rebuild No 46202 as a conventional machine.*

▲ *Treacy was acquainted with the railwaymen of Edge Hill shed before he took up photography. So the environs of the depot quickly became a favourite location. This c 1938 view shows a mixture of passenger and freight types, mostly LMS built. The engines from left to right are a Princess Royal Pacific, Jubilee class 4–6–0 No 5601 British Guiana, two class 4 0–6–0s Nos 4180 and 3908, LMS class 4P compound 4–4–0 No 1160 and a rebuilt Claughton 4–6–0 No 5946 Duke of Connaught.*

▶ *The former 'Turbomotive' No 46202 emerged from Crewe works as a conventional Pacific in August 1952 and was named* Princess Anne. *Treacy caught up with her on Merseyside in the late summer and took a number of shots including this view outside Edge Hill shed. On 8 October 1952 the engine was involved in the terrible double collision at Harrow & Wealdstone. It never worked again; although official withdrawal did not come until May 1954 when its replacement, the equally unique, BR standard class 8 Pacific No 71000* Duke of Gloucester *was taken into traffic. The foreground gives a marvellous view of the spartan footplate of LNWR 0–8–0 No 49355.*

◀ *The crew of class 3F 0–6–0 tank No 47519 have time for a quiet chat in a forgotten corner of Edge Hill shed, adjacent to the turntable, oblivious to the photographer or to the trains rumbling overhead. Judging by the coal in the bunker and on the cab roof they are running round having just visited the nearby coaling stage.*

▲ *Princess Coronation class 4–6–2 No 6254* City of Stoke on Trent, *in post-war LMS lined black livery, receives attention on Edge Hill shed prior to returning south with an express for London. A Crewe North based class 5 4–6–0 No 5025, now preserved on Strathspey Railway, also awaits its next turn of duty on the right.*

▶ *This portrait of Patriot class 4–6–0 No 5523 is taken from an unusual but very effective angle. The Edge Hill cleaners have provided an immaculate finish to the late 1930s style LMS crimson red livery, although the engine is obviously not long out of the shops. It was named* Bangor *in 1938, shortly after this picture was taken. An LNWR 0–8–0 stands on the left.*

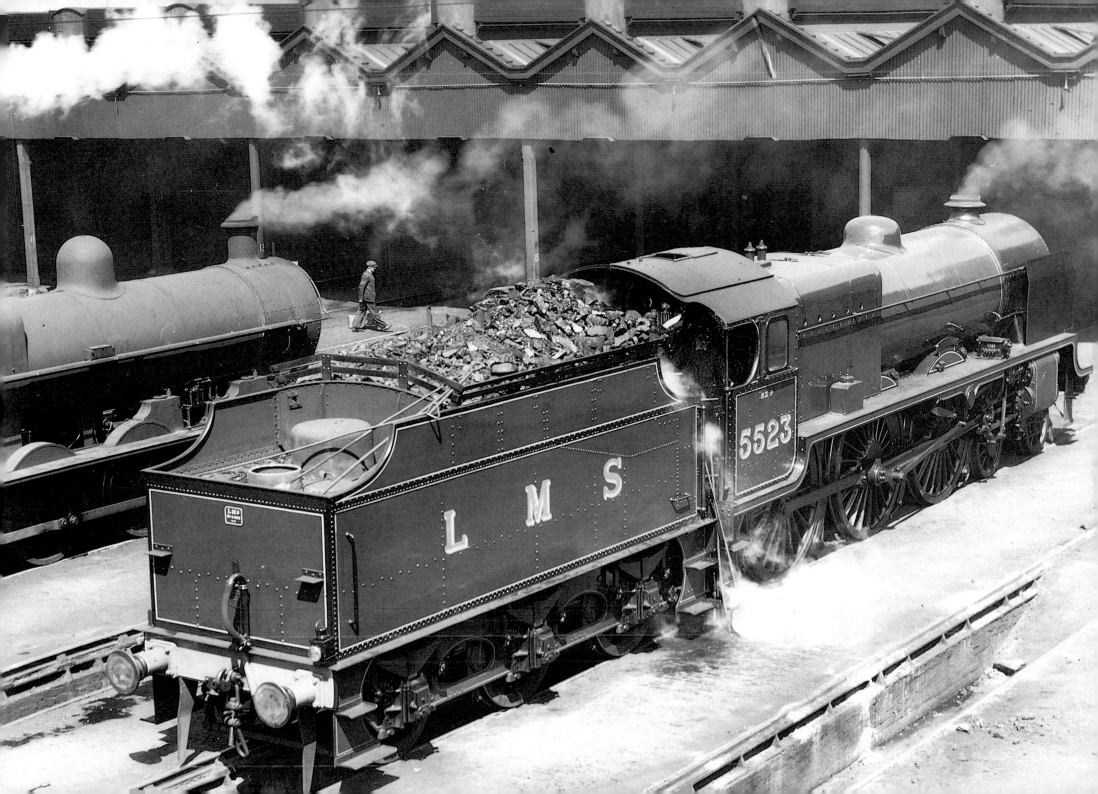

CHESTER–HOLYHEAD

◄ *A Stanier version of the class 5 2–6–0 No 42961 departs from Chester with an early evening express for Birkenhead c 1949. The line from Chester to Birkenhead was jointly owned by the LMS and GWR prior to nationalisation. The train reflects this, containing a mixture of both companies' stock. A GWR Siphon G leads the rake.*

▲ *An up Great Western route express for Shrewsbury departs Chester General behind Churchward veteran Star class 4–6–0 No 4013* Knight of St. Patrick. *Two more GWR engines are visible on the shed. Although probably taken after nationalisation there is no evidence of any change of ownership in this picture.*

▶ LMS class 5 4–6–0 No 44742, allocated to Llandudno Junction, is leaving Llandudno station with a Manchester express in the summer of 1948. Fitted with Caprotti valve gear, No 44742 was built under BR auspices in 1948. There were over 1500 locomotives built to company/regional designs during BR days, compared with only 999 steam locomotives built to BR standard designs.

◀ The mountains of North Wales provide a backdrop for this view of LNWR class G2a 0–8–0 No 49291 on a local Llandudno-Bangor train at Bethesda Junction c 1949. This freight engine, based at Mold Junction, was an unusual sight on a passenger service. It may well have been 'borrowed' by Llandudno Junction shed due to a shortage of available motive power on a busy summer afternoon.

▶ A classic pre-war shot of the up Irish Mail speeding along the North Wales coast main line at Bethesda Junction. Class 2P 4-4-0 No 655 pilots a Royal Scot, probably No 6112 Sherwood Forester. *In 1939 the day train left Holyhead at 12.40pm and arrived in London Euston at 5.50pm. Note the Post Office sorting coach second in the rake.*

◀ Another crisp pre-war view shows LMS class 5 4-6-0 No 5346 passing Penryn sidings, near Bangor, at the head of a Bangor to Chester stopping train c 1938. The locomotive was built by Armstrong Whitworth in 1937.

◀ *An up express hauled by Patriot class 4–6–0 No 45504 Royal Signals leaves Bangor and is about to dive into the monumental Egyptian style portal of Bangor tunnel at the east end of the station. The picture was taken in the early to mid 1950s.*

▲ *An elderly L&Y class 3F 0–6–0 No 52119 performs shunting duties in Bangor station in the early 1950s. No 52119 was already 60 years old when this picture was taken and still had another 10 years service ahead of it. Surely a healthy return on the original investment.*

A handsome portrait of rebuilt Royal Scot class 4–6–0 No 46112 Sherwood Forester *standing at its home depot of Holyhead in the early 1950s. No 46112 left Holyhead in February 1953 and was reallocated to Leeds Holbeck a few weeks later after a period on loan. Treacy had even more opportunities to photograph it in West Yorkshire.*

▶ *Another rebuilt Royal Scot No 46127* The Old Contemptibles *makes a meal of the steep gradient out of Holyhead station courtesy of the fireman. It was rebuilt with taper boiler and double chimney in 1944. All the rebuilds eventually received smoke deflectors. This 1948 view shows the engine, in BR black with LNWR style lining, working the up Irish Mail. Holyhead depot is on the right.*

PRESTON AND LANCASTER

Treacy did not find much inspiration amongst the open countryside of the southern sections of the west coast route. Even close to home in Lancashire it was in the environs of the major stations where he found most to interest him.

▲ The up Coronation Scot approaches Boar's Head, north of Wigan, headed by streamlined Princess Coronation class Pacific No 6223 Princess Alice. The up and down trains were booked to pass at Preston, thus a visit to Boar's Head in the late afternoon would enable both services to be seen speeding by.

▶ A Royal Scot class 4–6–0 No 6162 Queen's Westminster Rifleman crosses the river Ribble south of Preston with an up ordinary passenger service comprising two three-coach non-corridor sets c 1937. The LNWR signal gantries and the track gang in the distance add to this superb composition.

▲ A Fowler 2–6–4T leaves Preston for Blackpool under another fine array of signals, note the LNWR arms have now been replaced by upper quadrants. This picture was taken when No 42317 was based at Springs Branch shed, Wigan during 1960/1. The coaches are all BR Mk1s in maroon livery. During the season there were through trains and coaches to Blackpool from all over the country, together with innumerable excursions.

▶ LMS built compound class 4P 4–4–0 No 1192 gathers speed as it leaves Preston with a southbound express, probably for Liverpool Exchange, in the late 1930s. The compound is based at Bank Hall shed (23A) in Liverpool, which had been the principal L&Y shed in the city.

◄ The vast majority of freight operations during the steam era used wagons and vans which were not fitted with continuous brakes, this inevitably meant they could only be worked at relatively low speeds. The first view shows a superheated ex-L&Y 0–6–0 No 12619 hauling an up freight south of Preston running under the mineral or empty wagon code. It was taken in the late 1930s.

▶ The full page view was taken at Carnforth some fifteen years later. A Stanier class 5 4–6–0 No 45348 makes light work of a southbound express freight, which despite its name still did not have to contain any fitted vehicles. The twin coaling tower and ash disposal plant of Carnforth locomotive depot can be seen to the left.

◀ Lancaster Castle and the Priory gave an excellent backdrop to Treacy's pictures of southbound trains tackling the 1 in 98 gradient out of the main line station – also known as Lancaster Castle. A BR standard class 6 4–6–2 No 72000 Clan Buchanan blasts its way up the bank as it restarts a Glasgow to Manchester express c 1957.

▲ A Fowler class 4 2–6–4 tank No 42301 stands at Lancaster Castle station with a local passenger train. The engine was based at Oxenholme during the 1950s, a shed normally associated with banking duties up to Grayrigg. The non-corridor coach is of LNWR origin.

The main picture features Coniston station, the delightful terminus of a branch line from Foxfield, in the heart of the southern Lakes. An Ivatt class 2 2–6–2 tank No 41217 provides motive power for the single-coach push-pull service. The branch was a pre-Beeching casualty, closing in October 1958.

A Carlisle Upperby based Patriot class 4–6–0 No 45502 *Royal Naval Division leaves Oxenholme with a short five-coach up express c 1951. This was the junction for the Windermere branch. Although an important passenger station, particularly for tourist traffic, this rural area required only primitive goods facilities.*

TRANS-PENNINE

◀ *The Lancashire & Yorkshire line between Manchester and Leeds was the original trans-Pennine route. Engineered by* George Stephenson, it followed the Calder valley through the West Riding. In this classic Pennine mill town scene BR standard class 5 4–6–0 No 73044 pulls away from Sowerby Bridge station with an eastbound Liverpool Exchange - Newcastle express in the mid 1950s.

▲ *At the other end of town an incredibly neat rake of Stanier coaches forms a westbound express for Liverpool headed by a Stanier class 5 4–6–0 No 44823.*

▲ At the top of the climb LMS Jubilee class 4–6–0 No 45705 Seahorse approaches the eastern portal of Standedge tunnel with the morning Hull–Liverpool restaurant car express, c 1955. The class O8 diesel shunter is on the up slow line which leads into one of the two early single-bore tunnels, now disused. The Huddersfield narrow canal also pierces the Pennines at this point.

▶ The firemen are working hard as this Newcastle–Liverpool express pounds up the bank, near Geldholt, from Huddersfield to Standedge tunnel. A Manchester based unrebuilt Patriot No 45520 Llandudno heads the train, piloting another 4–6–0 in the form of a Stanier class 5.

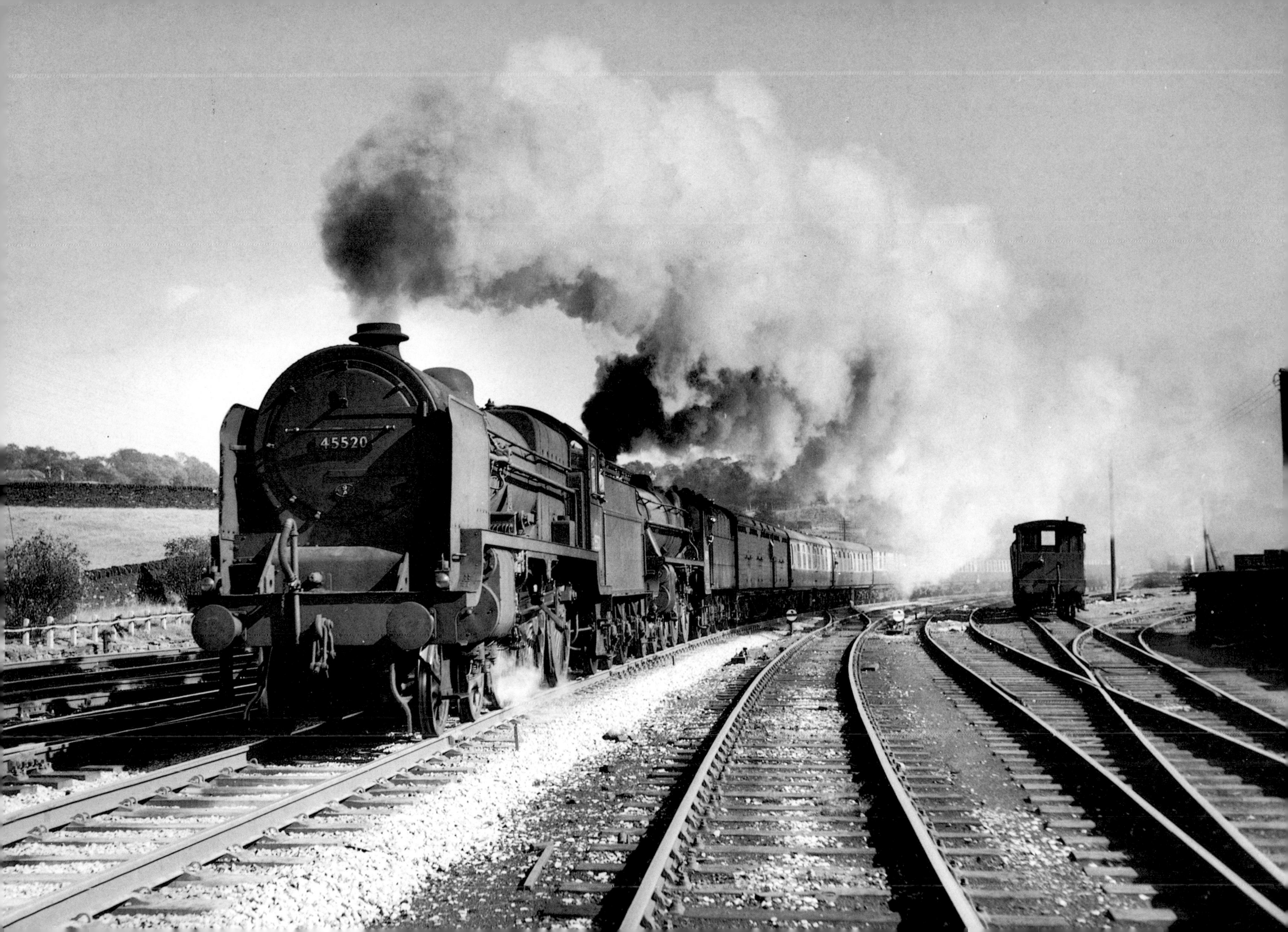
45520

◀ *An LMS Fowler class 7F 0–8–0 No 49674 trundles through the pleasant wooded country along the Calder valley, near Hebden Bridge, with a train of coal empties for the Yorkshire coalfield. The last of 175 examples of the design, it was built in July 1932. The tower of Heptonstall church can be seen on the skyline.*

▶ *The accompanying picture was taken some twenty miles further east along the L&Y main line. A War Department 2–8–0 No 90076 hauls a short freight through Horbury cutting c 1966. The end of steam in this part of the world was not very far away by this date. In the background the floodlights of Healey Mills marshalling yard are visible.*

◄ Rebuilt Patriot class 4–6–0 No 45535 Sir Herbert Walker K.C.B. passes Bradley Junction signal box, near Huddersfield, with the 9.00am Liverpool–Newcastle express. To the right a class 5 Mogul No 42920 drifts along the slow line with a short through freight. The curve off to the right connected with the L&Y main line to the west, at Bradley Wood Junction.

▲ A veteran LMS-built compound 4–4–0 No 41188 leads the way as a Hull to Liverpool express hauled by class 5 4–6–0 No 45340 forges west up the 1 in 112 gradient past Linthwaite Goods. The picture was taken in the spring of 1954 or 1955 when the much travelled compound had spells of duty working out of Farnley Junction shed (25G). By the end of 1955 it had been withdrawn.

▲ A class 5 2–6–0 No 42862 takes a relief express westwards over the Pennines. Although chiefly employed on freight duties the Horwich Moguls were often called upon to work passenger duties at peak periods. The Wakefield (56A) based engine is passing Linthwaite around 1957/8.

LUNE GORGE

Three pictures taken at Grayrigg on the same day in the summer of 1959.

◀ *Princess Royal class 4–6–2 No 46211* Queen Maud *passes the disused platforms of Grayrigg station – closed in 1954 – with a Glasgow to Birmingham express. The track gang are working on the up main line.*

▶ *The accompanying views show two down trains. An Oxenholme banker assists a freight of tank wagons up the last few yards of the bank, the class 4 2–6–4T is probably No 42613.*

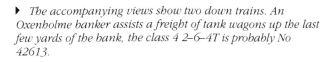

▶ *In the next shot the down Royal Scot heads for Glasgow with red liveried Princess Coronation class Pacific No 46245* City of London *in charge. The banking engine has crossed the main line and waits in the up loop for the road back to Oxenholme. Note the surviving LNWR signals protecting the exit to the loop.*

▲ Low Gill station at the entrance to the Lune Gorge is the next port of call. An up express is headed by Liverpool based Patriot 4–6–0 No 45539 E.C. Trench c 1958. The picture was taken on a summer afternoon so it may be a Scotland to Liverpool working, running separately from the Manchester train. Note the train crew on the platform.

▶ The main photograph is a stunning landscape view featuring an up express on Dillicar troughs, south of Tebay. The rebuilt Royal Scot class 4–6–0 No 46121 Highland Light Infantry, City of Glasgow Regiment seems to have taken its fill as the water is overflowing out of the tank vents. The window ventilators in the leading carriage are still open, possibly giving somebody an unexpected soaking.

▲ The grandeur of the Lune Gorge scenery – before the coming of the motorway – is beautifully captured in this photograph. Notice how Treacy carefully waited until the class 5 was in the dip of the dry stone wall before pressing the shutter. The Stanier 4–6–0 No 45435 is heading up the main line with an express comprising LNER stock; probably a Saturdays Only Newcastle to Blackpool working.

▶ A class 4F 0–6–0 No 44292, allocated to Tebay shed, plods along the Lune Valley with a train of empty hoppers for north east England on a stormy early spring day. The wagon immediately behind the locomotive is of NER design.

SHAP

Treacy loved the Lake District and took holidays there over many years. At the eastern edge of the Lakes the west coast main line climbs to 916ft at Shap. This bleak stretch of line undoubtedly produced some of Treacy's finest work as the following pictures demonstrate.

▲ *Leaving Tebay. A forces special of mainly sheeted open wagons has taken the assistance of a class 4 2–6–4T as banker for the strenuous climb to Shap summit, four miles of which are graded at 1 in 75. The train engine, a Stanier class 8F No 48660 carries the special train reporting number hung from the smokebox handrail. In the distance the rake of hopper wagons is standing alongside the North Eastern branch from Kirby Stephen.*

▶ *Against the background of the Howgill Fells class 2P 4–4–0 No 40565 pilots BR standard 4–6–2 No 72004* Clan MacDonald, *with a heavy train for Glasgow, near Greenholme in the mid 1950s. The 2P will have joined the* Clan *at Preston, where portions from Liverpool and Manchester were united.*

▶ A chill westerly wind tugs at the exhaust of Patriot class 4–6–0 No 45542 and its banker as they approach the start of the 1 in 75 section of the climb to Shap summit with a down fitted freight. Once again the location is the road overbridge near Greenholme.

◀ In this pre-war view a rebuilt LNWR Claughton 4–6–0 No 6017 Breadalbane, of Carlisle Upperby shed, heads a down express freight climbing past Scout Green. The Claughtons were the final development in LNWR express passenger locomotive design. By the time this picture was taken, c 1937, withdrawal of the rebuilds was already underway.

▶ *Eric Treacy particularly treasured this picture of LMS Pacific No 6230* Duchess of Buccleuch *taken at Shap Wells in March 1942. The engine has just restarted its sixteen-coach load on the 1 in 75 gradient, having been held at Shap Wells signal. It is heading the 10.00am from Euston to Glasgow – the peacetime Royal Scot.*

◀ *An earlier, mid 1930s, view taken from the same position finds Royal Scot class 4–6–0 No 6156* The South Wales Borderer *making excellent progress up the bank with a down express. The class was rebuilt from 1943 onwards with taper boilers, transforming both their appearance and performance.*

◀ *This pair of photographs illustrates the same train pounding up the last few yards to Shap summit. The down express freight is headed by Stanier class 5 4–6–0 No 44833. Its BR number has been added without repainting.*

▶ *Bringing up the rear is Tebay banker No 2396, a Fowler class 4 2–6–4 tank, still in the short lived LMS livery of 1936/7. The date is around 1948/9.*

◄ The streamliner era LMS style. The pioneer LMS streamlined Pacific No 6220 Coronation *first appeared in 1937, designed to haul the new Coronation Scot service between London and Glasgow. Five locomotives were painted blue with silver stripes to haul the matching nine coach sets. No 6220 is seen here in the first summer of operation tearing down the bank from Shap summit with the up train.*

▲ *Later batches of streamliners appeared in the more usual LMS crimson red colours, coupled with gold stripes. Illustrated here by No 6227* Duchess of Devonshire *hauling an up express at Thrimby Grange, on the northern ascent of Shap, in the late summer of 1938.*

▶ *A true LNWR workhorse. Super D 0–8–0 No 9120 trundles south with a through freight at Eden Valley Junction, near Penrith, in the late 1930s. This engine started life as a four-cylinder compound, built around the turn of the century. It has just been rebuilt to its final form, class G2a, and remained in service until 1959.*

◀ *Rebuilt Scot No 46102* Black Watch *shatters the restful atmosphere of Shap station as it sweeps a northbound express down the bank towards Penrith. Everything is tidy and orderly, not even a stone out of place on the gravel topped up platform. Shap station closed in 1968. Dr Beeching disapproved of main line stopping services, especially those serving rural areas.*

◀ *Hughes class 5 2–6–0 No 42940 of Crewe South shed catches the evening sunshine as it climbs Shap bank with a northbound freight in the mid 1950s. This was the most successful design to appear during the turbulent early years of the London, Midland & Scottish Railway.*

◀ *Two grime laden locomotives thread their way through Strickland woods on the southbound ascent to Shap. A class 5 4–6–0 No 45351 leads a Jubilee 4–6–0, probably No 45665* Lord Rutherford of Nelson, *on an up express from Glasgow in 1960.*

▶ *A Rebuilt Scot 4–6–0 No 46135* The East Lancashire Regiment *climbs through the woods near Great Strickland with an up express, c 1958. Around this time the livery for corridor coaches was changing from red and cream to maroon.*

The market town of Penrith was an important railway junction, which in the 1930s and 40s provided a fascinating mixture of the old and the new. The west coast main line played host to streamlined expresses, while the Cockermouth, Keswick & Penrith and the NER line to Kirkby Stephen and beyond into County Durham provided cross-country trains hauled by venerable relics of Victorian design.

▶ The main picture, taken after the war, shows a sixteen-coach Glasgow to Manchester and Liverpool express at the south end of Penrith. It is headed by Newton Heath based Jubilee class 4–6–0 No 5711 *Courageous*, with piloting assistance provided by LMS built class 2P 4–4–0 No 652 of Carlisle Upperby shed.

◀ An exiled Great Eastern Intermediate 2–4–0 No 7416 (classified E4 by the LNER) sets out from Penrith, with a rake of NER clerestory coaches, for Darlington. After connecting with a train from Tebay at Kirkby Stephen it will face the climb over Stainmore to Barnard Castle.

◀ The pristine condition of non-streamlined Princess Coronation class Pacific No 6232 Duchess of Montrose suggests it is only a few weeks old in this late 1930s view. It was turned out of Crewe works in July 1938 and is already hard at work on the up Midday Scot, just south of Penrith.

SETTLE & CARLISLE

Treacy found the Midland line up the Aire valley from Leeds was easily accessible, especially when he was based in Keighley. Many of his finest photographs of the early post-war scene were taken along this route.

▲ This rare view shows the down Flying Scotsman passing Marley Junction, near Keighley, probably on 16 August 1948. Following extensive flood damage the east coast main line in south east Scotland was closed from 13 August. The Waverley route was also blocked for a brief period. Therefore on 14 and 16 August the Flying Scotsman was diverted via Selby to Leeds, over the Settle & Carlisle and on to Edinburgh via Carstairs. Still in LNER guise class A4 Pacific No 25 Falcon heads the train of 'teak' liveried stock. The east coast route did not reopen for passenger traffic until 1 November 1948.

▶ An up freight of coal empties rumbles past Skipton South Junction box in the late 1950s with an early LMS, right hand drive, class 4F 0–6–0 No 44041 in charge. The overbridge carries the lines from Ilkley and Grassington into Skipton.

◀ *Several of the newly rebuilt Royal Scots were allocated to Holbeck shed and Treacy was soon admiring their powerful lines. No 6108* Seaforth Highlander *– rebuilt in August 1943 – pauses at Hellifield station with a down express c 1947. It carries the post-war LMS livery of black lined out with maroon and straw.*

▶ *One of the popular L&Y 2–4–2 tanks No 10899 is caught here at Hellifield, its home depot, c 1947. This example, built in 1910, was a Hughes development of the original Aspinall design and was withdrawn in October 1948.*

Surprisingly Treacy did not start photographing on the Settle & Carlisle route until the 1950s, but he soon found the Long Drag irresistible, with its combination of wild mountain scenery and spectacularly engineered viaducts and tunnels.

▲ A BR built Fairburn 2–6–4 tank No 42051 leaves Settle station with an up local train, comprising a three-coach non-corridor set. The date is around 1959.

▶ This marvellous 1950s period piece was taken from the signal box at Garsdale station. A rebuilt Royal Scot 4–6–0 No 46112 Sherwood Forester speeds north with a Glasgow express. The North Eastern branch to Hawes and Northallerton curves away on the right hand side.

▶ The whole sweep of the landscape at Ribblehead is beautifully caught in this picture, with the sharp outline of Pen y Ghent to the left and the slopes of Ingleborough dominating the right. Above, white clouds drift across a remarkably friendly sky. Through all this splendid scenery a Midland class 4F plods north between Ribblehead viaduct and Blea Moor tunnel with an engineer's train.

◀ Still in filthy LMS livery Holbeck (20A) based Royal Scot No 46117 Welsh Guardsman climbs the last mile of 1 in 100 grade to Ais Gill summit around 1950. It was on this locomotive that Treacy made his first post-war footplate trip. The leading coach in this up express has probably been added as a strengthener.

▲ A WD class 8F 2–8–0 No 90359 approaches Blea Moor signal box with the Long Meg anhydrite empties around 1958. Neat trains of hopper wagons on a dedicated working were something of a rarity at this time.

▶ A Carlisle Kingmoor allocated class 5 2–6–0 No 42780 slowly but surely treks up the bank to Ais Gill with a southbound tanker train. The unmistakable shape of Wild Boar Fell provides the backdrop.

◀ *Treacy took two of these shots by climbing a signal post at Dent station. The main picture shows a* BR Britannia class Pacific No 70053 Moray Firth *at the head of the northbound* Thames-Clyde Express *c 1957. Arten Gill viaduct can be seen in the distance.*

▶ *Looking the other way reveals the layout of the highest main line station in England. On the up line a class 5 2–6–0 No 42774 drifts down hill with a through freight. Note the snow fences on the hillside to the right.*

▶ *Back on terra firma. An Ivatt class 4 2–6–0 No 43139 has shunted back 'across the road' at Dent with a short engineer's train of dropside wagons. This view was taken in 1966/7 when steam power on anything but the most lowly task was becoming rare.*

CARLISLE

Main lines approached the border city of Carlisle from almost every point of the compass, bringing a wide variety of famous locomotives and trains into the gothic splendour of Citadel Joint station. Treacy found plenty of subject matter both in the station area and at Upperby and Kingmoor sheds.

▶ *A pair of LMS 4–6–0s head a Glasgow-Manchester express out of Carlisle in 1960. Patriot class No 45502* Royal Naval Division *of Upperby shed acts as pilot to an unknown Jubilee.*

◀ *The penultimate Princess Coronation class 4–6–2 No 46256* Sir William A. Stanier F.R.S. *draws out of Carlisle with a Perth to London Euston express in the early 1950s. To the left a Carnforth based 2–6–4 tank No 42428 waits to take a train south via the Cumbrian coastal route.*

◀ *Jubilee 4–6–0 No 45728* Defiance *passes Durran Hill Junction with the up Waverley express for London St Pancras in the late 1950s. The St Pancras to Edinburgh service was named* The Waverley *in 1957. The eight-coach formation includes an LMS twelve-wheel restaurant car.*

◄ The large number of companies which operated into Carlisle in the pre-Grouping era left subsequent organisations with a complex series of freight yards. All these yards required goods wagons to be tripped between them before going on to their ultimate destination. Here a Caledonian class 3F 0–6–0 No 57621 passes Bog Junction, Carlisle with trip working No K5 around 1949.

▶ This equally traditional scene at Upperby sidings shows a class 5 4–6–0 No 45386 of Barrow shed departing with a partially fitted freight. The only concessions to modern operation are the diesel shunters visible to the left of the train. The engines to the right are stabled at Upperby shed.

▲ The sunlight throws kaleidoscopic shadows across the south end of Citadel station as a BR standard Clan class Pacific awaits departure with an up express in the mid 1950s. The driver of No 72001 Clan Cameron is checking the oil level in the connecting rod big end.

▶ Engine change at Carlisle in the mid 1950s. Camden based Princess Coronation class Pacific No 46244 King George VI has brought the down Royal Scot into Citadel station from Euston. Sister engine No 46231 Duchess of Atholl, allocated to Polmadie, will take over for the rest of the journey to Glasgow.

▶ *Polmadie based Princess Coronation No 46221* Queen Elizabeth *stands at the north end of Carlisle awaiting the right away with the 11.15am Birmingham to Glasgow service. This early 1950s view shows the locomotive in BR blue livery. Also worthy of note is the sloping top to the smokebox a legacy of its streamlined days.*

◀ *A Fowler class 4 2–6–4 tank eases away from Carlisle with a northbound train c 1961. Although running under express lights the train contains some non-corridor stock. In the background a class 3F 0–6–0 tank No 47515 is on station pilot duty.*

◀ Both engine and train still display LNER livery in this c 1949 view of Thompson class B1 4–6–0 No 61221 Sir Alexander Erskine-Hill *departing the north end of Carlisle with an afternoon stopping train for Edinburgh via the Waverley route.*

▲ *A Gresley class A3 Pacific No 60087* Blenheim *reverses onto its train in platform 3 of Citadel station. The Haymarket based locomotive will head the express, from London St* Pancras, to Edinburgh over the Waverley route. The platform is packed with rarities in comparison with today's scene, parcels trolleys, packing cases and even porters.

▲ A Stanier class 5 4–6–0 No 45121, of Motherwell shed, pulls an up freight through Floriston woods in the border country.

▲ Gretna Junction just north of the border was the bifurcation point of the Glasgow & South Western and Caledonian main lines. Still just in Scotland a through freight heads south on the Caledonian line hauled by class 5 2–6–0 No 42912. The picture was taken in the late 1950s.

◄ The down Thames Clyde express crosses the river Eden north of Carlisle with a Royal Scot class 4–6–0 No 46109 Royal Engineer in command. The Leeds Holbeck allocated engine will work through to Glasgow St Enoch via the GSWR route.

BEATTOCK

Like Shap to the south, Beattock provided a formidable obstacle for the heavy Anglo-Scottish traffic. Again it was the northbound ascent which provided the stiffest test and so it was here that Treacy tended to concentrate his efforts, despite difficulties with the light.

▶ *A Stanier class 5 4–6–0 No 44953, with banking engine at the rear, starts the long climb hauling a northbound fitted freight on a glorious summer evening in the late 1950s.*

◀ *The early morning mist has not yet cleared as Stanier Princess Royal class 4–6–2 No 46210* Lady Patricia *waits impatiently to be off with her northbound express, a sleeper from Euston, in the late 1950s. A Caledonian 0–4–4 tank shunts by the locomotive shed.*

◀ *The stone built two-road locomotive shed at Beattock housed the banking engines which assisted northbound trains. Here a brace of LMS class 4 2–6–4 tanks, with BR built No 42192 to the fore, await their next turn of duty. The shed closed in 1967.*

▶ A Fairburn 2–6–4 tank No 42205 provides an elegant broadside portrait as it drifts down the bank towards Beattock having assisted a train up the bank. The engine carries BR lined black livery with the later symbol applied.

◀ Grangemouth (65F) based class 5 2–6–0 No 42780 struggles up the 1 in 74 at Harthope with a down through freight, which includes military vehicles. A column of steam from the hard working banking engine can be seen at the rear of the train.

◀ The towering exhaust of Princess Coronation class Pacific No 46223 Princess Alice *echoes around the hills as she climbs the gradient near Greskine. It is a summer morning in 1960 and the Polmadie (66A) based engine is in charge of the* 12.20am Euston–Glasgow Central sleeping car service. Extra coaches will have been added at Carlisle, including a restaurant car to provide breakfast. At the rear of this ensemble an LMS 2–6–4 tank provides assistance.

▲ Another early morning shot at a similar location finds Carlisle Kingmoor based class 5 2–6–0 No 42830 tackling the gradient with a through freight. A Fairburn 2–6–4 tank acts as banker at the rear of this interesting assortment of wagons.

The next few photographs are all taken on the steepest section of the climb, around 1 in 74/5 near Harthope, and capture the cream of LMS motive power attacking the gradient.

◀ *Princess Royal class 4–6–2 No 46203* Princess Margaret Rose *heads a neat rake of Stanier coaches forming the 11.15am Birmingham-Glasgow express in August 1952. The locomotive still carries an original domeless boiler.*

▶ *Springtime snow still clings to the mountains in this view of a former streamlined Pacific No 46222* Queen Mary *working hard on the down Royal Scot c 1958.*

◀ *A set of newly introduced BR Mk1 coaches was provided for the Royal Scot in the summer of 1952. The locomotive heading the train is a non-streamlined Princess Coronation No 46250* City of Lichfield, *in early BR blue livery. It was repainted green in February of 1953, therefore this picture must have been taken in the late summer of 1952, when the 10.00am from Euston was due in Glasgow at 6.00pm.*

▶ *This picture was also taken in the late afternoon; possibly on the same day. Former streamlined Princess Coronation, note the sloping top to the smokebox, No 46227* Duchess of Devonshire *climbs the bank unassisted with an eleven coach express, probably from Birmingham.*

▶ *This last view of Beattock shows the southbound ascent near Crawford. Princess Coronation class 4–6–2 No 46223* Princess Alice *is having no difficulty with the fourteen-coach up Royal Scot. The date is 1957 or 58 as most of the stock is now painted in maroon livery. Note the Caledonian style catch-point notice.*

SCOTLAND

▲ *Carstairs, junction for Edinburgh. Rebuilt Scot No 46107 Argyll and Sutherland Highlander draws a northbound express out of the station c 1957/8. A typical Caledonian lattice post signal stands in the foreground, although the arms are LMS replacements.*

▶ *On the GSWR main line. BR Britannia class 4–6–2 No 70044 Earl Haig passes Dumfries shed as it leaves the station with the up Thames Clyde express in the late 1950s. Another BR standard, a class 5 4–6–0, simmers on the shed. To its right is a Caledonian 0–6–0T.*

▶ A BR standard class 4 2–6–4 tank No 80001 stands in platform 8 of Glasgow Central station with a local train, for main line stations, in the late 1950s. The engine carries a Caledonian style route indicator on its central bufferbeam lamp bracket. Above, the signal gantry still has lower quadrant arms.

◀ A typical robust Caledonian design, class 3F 0–6–0 No 57626 hauls a loaded train of ballast hoppers through Uddingston Central station in the late 1950s.

Holidays in Scotland from the 1950s onwards allowed Treacy to get to know the scenic splendour of the Roads to the Isles. He recorded both the North British route from Glasgow to Fort William and Mallaig and the Highland line from Inverness and Dingwall to Kyle of Lochalsh.

◀ *No 61996* Lord of the Isles *was one of six three-cylinder K4 class locomotives built specially for the West Highland line by Sir Nigel Gresley. In this early 1950s view it is pounding up the grade through the twisting curves of the Monessie Gorge with an up freight. The waters of the river Spean tumble over the rocks immediately below.*

▶ *After nationalisation the ubiquitous LMS class 5s were soon drafted onto the West Highland line. No 45499 makes a spectacular start from Fort William station, hard against the shore of Loch Linnhe, with the morning train for Glasgow in the early 1950s.*

Just a short ferry ride away across the kyle the mountains of Skye form the backdrop to this busy Highland scene. LMS class 5 4–6–0 No 45179 is impatient to be away from Kyle of Lochalsh station with the early morning train to Inverness. At the quay the 1947 built MacBrayne ship MV Loch Seaforth is being tended by one of the dockside cranes before sailing to Mallaig.

Gresley's successor Edward Thompson reconstructed one of the K4s as a two cylinder machine. The rebuild class K1/1 No 61997 MacCailin Mor is seen here leaving Fort William with an up express for Glasgow Queen Street in the early 1950s. A GNR K2 2–6–0 and an NBR J36 0–6–0 stand in the goods yard.

▲ A Gresley class V1 2–6–2 tank No 67610 enters Dalmeny station, at the south end of the Forth Bridge, with an up local train for Edinburgh. Note the wooden section of platform used to save weight on the bridge.

▶ BR standard class 5 4–6–0 No 73152 rumbles across the massive structure of the Forth Bridge with an up local train c 1958. The St Rollox based locomotive was one of a series of 30 built with Caprotti valve gear by Derby works in the mid 1950s. The bridge, completed in 1890, was a joint venture financed largely by English railway companies.

When the much lamented Waverley route closed in 1969 not only was a useful through route lost but many small towns in southern Scotland were also left miles from the railway network. Speeds were never great on this meandering saw-tooth route which included two gruelling climbs to Whitrope and Falahill summits.

◄ Treacy rarely photographed on wet days, preferring the better contrast provided by the sunlight. However there is still plenty of life in this shot of LNER B1 4 6 0 No 61191 passing through Galashiels station in the 1950s with an up partially fitted freight service.

► The lonely outpost of Falahill box over 800ft up in the Moorfoot hills is illustrated here, with a K3 class 2–6–0 No 61876 slogging up the last few yards to the summit with a down fitted freight in the late 1950s.

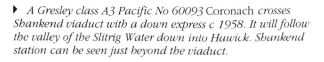

► A Gresley class A3 Pacific No 60093 Coronach crosses Shankend viaduct with a down express c 1958. It will follow the valley of the Slitrig Water down into Hawick. Shankend station can be seen just beyond the viaduct.

EDINBURGH

The two main sheds in Edinburgh were St Margarets and Haymarket, both former NBR and LNER depots. St Margarets had the larger allocation, but Haymarket housed the Pacifics for the most important east coast main line work.

▶ *Class A4 4–6–2 No 60030* Golden Fleece, *now equipped with a double blast pipe and chimney, is being prepared for the top east coast service outside Haymarket shed; the* Elizabethan *was the non-stop summer only service between London and Edinburgh. The date is 1961, the last year it was steam hauled.*

◀ *Peppercorn class A2 Pacific No 60537* Bachelor's Button *is turned, using the vacuum operated turntable, at Haymarket depot in the mid 1950s. It had a relatively short existence, only fourteen years, ten of which were spent working out of Haymarket.*

◀ *The cramped and smoky site of St Margarets shed is well illustrated in this 1950s view. The depot straddled the main line to the east of Edinburgh and had to cater for one of the largest allocations of locomotives in the country. The majority of engines on shed in this view are still ex-LNER types. A class K2 2–6–0 No 61789 heads west on the down main line.*

◀ *The up Queen of Scots keeps to the main line as it passes Portobello East junction – where the Waverley route leaves for Carlisle – in the mid 1950s. The beautifully presented Haymarket class A3 Pacific No 60090 Grand Parade is already well notched-up and showing a clean exhaust at the head of the eight-car Pullman set.*

▶ *The fortress-like retaining walls make an impressive entrance to the east end of Edinburgh Waverley station from Calton Hill tunnel. North British class J37 0–6–0 No 64622 proceeds slowly over the crossings with a down coal train, running under through freight lamps.*

▶ *Waverley east end departure. Class A3 No 60090* Grand Parade *pulls away from the station with the up Queen of Scots in the mid 1950s. This locomotive was a replacement for the engine with the same name and LNER number, 2744, which was wrecked in the Castlecary accident of December 1937.*

◀ *The mid-day departure from Edinburgh Waverley, the up* Queen of Scots, *accelerates away from the platform with Peppercorn class A2 4–6–2 No 60536* Trimbush *in charge.*

◀ *King's Cross based A4 No 60022* Mallard *sparkles in the morning sunshine as it prepares to depart on its non-stop journey to London with the up* Elizabethan. *The date is around 1960. The coaches on the opposite platform are also for London. They form the up* Waverley *express, travelling via Carlisle and Leeds, to London St Pancras.*

◀ The fireman damps down the coal in the GNR tender of No 60041 Salmon Trout to prevent dust flying everywhere. He is using the station water supply, generally used for filling carriage water tanks. The class A3 Pacific is heading an afternoon departure from the west end of Waverley station, probably for Glasgow, in the summer of 1957.

▲ West end departures. LNER class A1 Pacific No 60162 Saint Johnstoun and LMS class 5 4–6–0 No 44720 stand at the head of expresses for Aberdeen and Perth respectively. The vehicle behind No 44720 is a horse box, complete with groom's compartment. The date is 1954 or 55.

▶ *Class D11/2 4–4–0 No 62678* Luckie Mucklebackit *stands in Edinburgh Waverley station, with the 1.09pm express for Dundee, in the early 1950s. It was one of a series of these GCR designed engines built by the LNER for work in Scotland. They were given names associated with the novels of Sir Walter Scott.*

◀ *This overall view of the west end of Edinburgh Waverley station is dominated by the impressive outline of the North British Hotel. It must have seemed a rather brash building when new, given the Classical restraint which characterises much of the city's architecture. A sign of the railways' power and confidence during the Victorian age. A Gresley Pacific moves out of the station with a northbound express for Perth or Aberdeen.*

NEWCASTLE

▲ *A class V2 2–6–2 No 60978, of York shed, heads a southbound freight through Newcastle station in the mid 1950s. Treacy's vantage point for the opposite picture can be seen above the train.*

▶ *Church spires still dominate the skyline of this c 1960 view of Newcastle Central station. It was taken from the castle keep at the east end of the station; the lines on the left lead to the High Level bridge. An unknown Gresley Pacific negotiates the famous diamond crossings with northbound empty stock, whilst a North Eastern J72 0–6–0T stands as station pilot. Two LNER-designed North Tyneside electrics are also visible in platforms 1 and 2.*

◀ *Peppercorn class A1 4–6–2 No 60147 North Eastern,
appropriately based at Gateshead shed, slowly gathers speed
as it departs the west end of platform eight at Newcastle
Central c 1953. The visible coaches are post-war LNER designs
built specially for the Flying Scotsman service.*

▶ *Just a few yards up the track, under yet another impressive
NER signal gantry, Gresley class A3 Pacific No 60047
Donovan gingerly sets a southerly course with an express for
King's Cross – note the steam sanding gear in action. The
picture is probably dated around 1954.*

▶ *The semaphore signals give class A4 Pacific No 60019
Bittern the road as it exits Newcastle Central east end with
the down North Briton in 1952 or 53. The train was a
Leeds–Glasgow service, via the east coast main line, which
was named by BR in 1949.*

▶ Edinburgh Haymarket based class A4 4–6–2 No 60009 Union of South Africa *stands in Newcastle station with the down Flying Scotsman. The rather battered canopies give an excellent patina of light and shade to this c 1953 picture. The locomotive gained an excellent reputation on the top main line services and was subsequently preserved.*

◀ *A second bridge across the Tyne, named after King Edward VII, opened in 1906. It was placed at the west end of Newcastle Central allowing east coast main line trains to run through the station. A Peppercorn class A1 No 60138* Boswell *approaches the sharp curve at the south end of the bridge with the up Queen of Scots Pullman in the late 1950s.*

YORK

York has been one of England's key railway centres ever since the time of George Hudson, the 'Railway King'. After the war Treacy was soon photographing the seemingly endless procession of expresses which passed through the station under its graceful curving roof.

◄ *A Gresley class V2 2–6–2 No 60979 gently reverses onto its train at the north end of the station in 1949. The coaches are still in LNER varnished teak finish. To the left is a Peppercorn class A2 Pacific No 60531* Bahram.

▲ *A few minutes later LNER liveried Thompson class A2/3 No 60521* Watling Street *carefully gets to grips with the 1.00pm King's Cross to Newcastle express in order to avoid slipping as it leaves platform 9. The coaches are painted in an early BR experimental livery of chocolate and cream. On the right No 60979 is now ready to depart with a stopping train for Darlington.*

143

◄ *Shafts of sunlight stream through the train shed roof to illuminate this busy October 1956 scene. A London express has just arrived in platform 8 and passengers are hurrying for the exit or standing looking bewildered in front of the destination board, left foreground. The coaches of a cross-country service to Birmingham and Bristol are just visible in platform 3. To the right in platform 9 a class A1 Pacific heads an empty stock working.*

▶ *The mid-day York–Bristol express prepares to depart the south end bay platform, No 3, in the early 1950s. A Bristol Barrow Rd (22A) Jubilee No 45602* British Honduras *is in charge.*

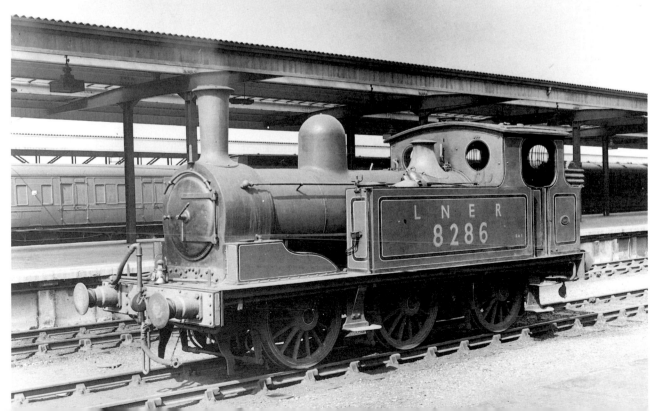

▶ *After the war the pilots at the major stations on the LNER system were repainted as a matter of priority. Resplendent in lined apple green livery J71 class 0–6–0 No 8286 awaits its next turn of duty at the south end of the station in the early days of nationalisation.*

◀ *In this bustling railway scene class A3 Pacific No 60092 Fairway leaves York with an up express in 1949. The station was undergoing resignalling around this time, replacing the North Eastern semaphores with colour light signals. The south end pilot, in the form of a J71 tank, is busy shunting to the right.*

▲ *Around eight years later, class A1 Pacific No 60114 W P Allen stands ready for the right away from platform 8 with a southbound express in 1957. All the coaches, including the catering vehicles, are BR Mk1s. The LMS stock on the right will form a cross-country service.*

▶ A Saltley based (21A) class 5 2–6–0 No 42790 heading south out of York with an ordinary passenger train is a rather unusual sight, particularly when the train consists exclusively of corridor stock. The combination is likely to be the 1.00pm for Sheffield.

◀ Two through freight trains come off the goods avoiding lines back onto the main line at Holgate Bridge Junction, south of York station, in the mid 1950s. On the left is class 04/5 No 63851 of Frodingham shed. To the right is a locally based engine, NER class B16/3 No 61464. Both were rebuilt with Gresley pattern boilers during LNER days. The roundhouse of York South shed is visible in the background.

◀ A class 8F 2–8–0 No 48119, hailing from Mansfield shed, pulls out of Dringhouses yard, south of York, with a through freight.

Two contrasting views at Holgate, York. The main picture shows apple green class A3 Pacific No 60092 Fairway heading the up Northumbrian in the summer of 1950. This King's Cross to Newcastle train was named by BR in 1949. A few years later the BR standard liveries have taken over completely in the photograph of LMS Jubilee class 4–6–0 No 45662 Kempenfelt leaving York with a Bristol express. However, as with the first view, the train is made up entirely from pre-nationalisation stock, in this case LMS. Note the semaphore signals have also disappeared. Both pictures show the wagons of a freight train on the left. It is possible that they show the same working as both trains are carrying iron ore. The older view shows the ore being carried in hopper wagons, whilst in the later version modern tippler wagons are being used.

▶ A York breakdown crane deals with a mishap near Queen St shed in the early days of nationalisation. It would appear that the NER class D20 4–4–0 could not decide which way to go through the turnout and therefore made an unfortunate compromise. The situation is obviously the focus of considerable debate. A B16 4–6–0 is in charge of the breakdown train.

◀ Jubilee class 4–6–0 No 45717 Dauntless stands on York North shed c 1949. The engine is still in LMS post-war black livery, although its BR number has been added in Gill Sans characters. The LMS power class 5XP is placed below the number.

◀ York North shed in the mid 1950s. An LMS Garratt 2–6–6–2 No 47967 peeps out from behind a line up of LNER Pacifics. From left to right they are Gresley class A3 No 60070 Gladiateur, Thompson class A2/3 No 60512 Steady Aim, Peppercorn class A1 No 60115 Meg Merrilies and a Thompson class A2/2.

YORKSHIRE

◀ *Gresley A3 Pacific No 60046* Diamond Jubilee *pauses at Wakefield Westgate station with the up White Rose, 3.15pm ex Leeds Central, for King's Cross. The locomotive is in the early British Railways' standard blue livery, carried by the most powerful express passenger classes. After only a few years this was superseded by dark Brunswick green. This helps to date the photograph to autumn 1951 or spring 1952.*

▶ *Hull Paragon station was a rare location for Eric Treacy. There are certainly no inclines to provide spectacular photographs. However, a typical bright, crisp Hull day helps to provide a suitable exhaust effect for this view of LNER class B1 4–6–0 No 61124 getting under way with an ordinary passenger train for Doncaster in the early to mid 1950s.*

▶ *Two WD 2–8–0s Nos 90321 and 90385 pass each other at Crofton, near Wakefield, whilst working coal trains in the mid 1960s. These Austerity engines had been built in large numbers during the war for military service. After the cessation of hostilities many were purchased, both by the LNER and subsequently BR, for freight work.*

LEEDS

Leeds Central station was a rather cramped and dismal terminus off Wellington Road. Yet it provided Treacy with an interesting variety of locomotives, all of which had to tackle a sharp 1 in 100 gradient as they started from the platform ends. The prestige services out of Central were the Pullmans and the GN Leeds-London expresses. The station closed in 1967.

▶ *The main picture shows the driver of Grantham based class A4 4–6–2 No 60026* Miles Beevor *giving a blast on the engine's mellow tri-toned whistle as it starts a London bound express in 1951. To the left is a class N1 0–6–2T No 69430.*

◀ *The last LNER Pacific design was the Peppercorn class A1. However, nationalisation had taken place before the first example appeared in August 1948. This dramatic view shows No 60123* H A Ivatt *leaving Leeds Central with an up express in 1952. Both locomotive and train are painted in the early BR standard colours, blue for No 60123 and red and cream for the coaches.*

▲ *An early evening shot of Leeds Central c 1954 shows LMS class 5 4–6–0 No 45216 leaving with an express for Liverpool via the L&Y route. It will be combined with a Bradford portion at Halifax. To the right LNER class A3 Pacific No 60055* Woolwinder *awaits departure with the 5.15pm express for London.*

▶ *Many of Treacy's best pictures at Leeds Central were taken around mid-day from the steps of the signalbox. In this view class A1 No 60123* H A Ivatt *provides the motive power once again. This time it is heading the 10.45am departure from Leeds Central, the Yorkshire Pullman, for King's Cross. The Harrogate and Bradford portions will have been combined here. The date is 1950 or 51.*

◄ *Peppercorn class A1 Pacific No 60131 Osprey heads the up Queen of Scots Pullman past Wortley South Junction, at the top of the initial climb out of Leeds Central, in the mid 1950s. This was another favourite Treacy location, especially during the afternoon as the up Queen of Scots departed Leeds at 4.35pm. The train ran from Glasgow and Edinburgh to King's Cross via Harrogate and Leeds. The front two cars would have been attached at Leeds to make the formation up to ten vehicles.*

▲ *An LMS Class 5 2–6–0 No 42876 hauls a southbound unfitted express freight through the disused platforms of Holbeck Low Level station around 1959. The Carlisle Kingmoor based engine is separated from the petrol tanks by barrier wagons, which were required for all dangerous freight cargoes. Two main lines to the north ran parallel here; the freight train is on the former Midland tracks, whilst those to the right formed the North Eastern route to Harrogate and beyond. Note the platelayer walking along the down road with hammer and shovel to hand.*

▶ *This shot was taken from the steps of Wortley Junction signal box in the mid 1950s. It shows one of Leeds Holbeck's allocation of rebuilt Royal Scot class 4–6–0s, No 46108* Seaforth Highlander, *working the down Thames-Clyde express out of Leeds. The bridge in the background carries the GN main line out of Leeds Central and immediately to its right is Holbeck High Level station.*

◀ *The up Thames-Clyde express pulls out of the Midland side of Leeds City station (formerly Wellington) with a class 5 4–6–0 No 44746, fitted with Caprotti valve gear, in charge. The north and southbound trains of this London St Pancras-Glasgow service departed Leeds within a few minutes of one another during this period of the early 1950s.*

◀ *All the BR standard locomotives had a distinctive 'house' style, which if it was not very aesthetically pleasing, was certainly functional. BR standard class 4 4–6–0 No 75062 leaves Leeds City with an ordinary passenger train for Bradford, conveying through coaches from Bristol on the last leg of their journey. It was allocated to Nottingham shed (16A) on completion at Swindon in May 1957. The picture was probably taken in 1958.*

Adjacent to the Midland terminus was the larger Leeds City train shed which was used by the trans-Pennine expresses. Engines changed here from London Midland to North Eastern Region examples and vice versa. With steep grades to tackle in both directions double heading was the norm. Something of the fascinating variety of combinations Treacy captured during the 1950s is presented here.

▶ A Newcastle–Liverpool service, after reversing, heads for Lancashire via Standedge tunnel. Patriot No 45519 Lady Godiva *pilots rebuilt Scot No 46124* London Scottish *past Leeds City West signal box in the mid 1950s.*

◀ In the opposite direction a Newcastle bound train leaves Leeds City c 1958. A class A3 Pacific No 60074 Harvester *is assisted by a Hunt class 4–4–0 No 62749* The Cottesmore *for the climb up to Harrogate. Both are Leeds Neville Hill based engines. Only the Queens Hotel is recognisable from this scene today.*

◀ Steam roars impatiently from the safety valves of LNER class B1 4–6–0 No 61016 Inyala *as it awaits the right away from Leeds City. It is piloting a class V2 2–6–2 on a Liverpool–Newcastle express, around 1957/8.*

▶ *A Patricroft (10C) allocated LMS class 5 4–6–0 No 45424 is about to depart with a trans-Pennine express in the early 1950s. Whilst the LNER is represented by class D49/2 4–4–0 No 62738 The Zetland, shrouded in steam as it awaits a working back to its home depot of Starbeck, Harrogate (50D).*

◀ *An early LMS-built compound 4–4–0, with right hand drive, No 41067 stands in the small servicing area adjacent to Leeds City station. It is painted in BR lined black livery and has a small version of the BR symbol on the tender. From the Royal Scot with the Coat of Arms headboard in the background, carried to celebrate the Coronation, the picture can be dated to 1953.*

GRANTHAM

◀ *In contrast to the photograph above, this rebuilt Great Eastern class B12/3 4–6–0 No 61565 is relatively clean in its BR lined black livery. It is heading a stopping train for Peterborough, at Little Ponton, south of Grantham c 1950.*

▲ *An up freight emerges from Peascliffe tunnel, on the east coast main line north of Grantham. It is hauled by a Gresley three-cylinder 2–8–0 No 63923, classified O2/1. By the time this picture was taken in the late 1940s or early 1950s the external condition of freight locomotives was largely ignored, although someone at Peterborough's New England depot has wiped the tender and cabside to reveal the number and British Railways' branding beneath the grime.*

LONDON – KING'S CROSS

▶ *The original Gresley streamlined class A4 Pacific No 60014* Silver Link, *built to haul the* Silver Jubilee *in the mid 1930s, and now in BR guise, finds work on another prestige service, the Yorkshire Pullman, c 1952/3. The train left King's Cross at 5.30pm and conveyed coaches for Hull and Bradford as well as Leeds and Harrogate.*

◀ *This view was taken towards the end of steam's reign on the east coast expresses. Already diesels can be seen lurking in the background. A Peppercorn class A1 4–6–2 No 60130* Kestrel, *of Copley Hill shed, Leeds, returns north with an evening express in 1963.*

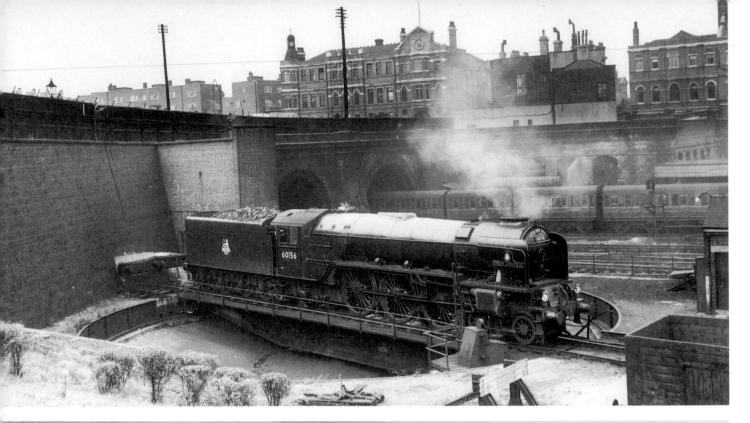

▶ King's Cross in 1949. Newly built class A1 Pacific No 60133 (later named Pommern) stands at the head of the 10.00am service for Edinburgh Waverley, the Flying Scotsman. One can almost sense the excitement and anticipation as departure time draws near. Meanwhile on more mundane duties a gaggle of class N2 0–6–2 tanks take care of the suburban traffic. The impressive outline of St Pancras station dominates the skyline.

◀ A small servicing area was provided adjacent to King's Cross station to avoid too many light engine movements up to King's Cross shed proper. The turntable was crammed in, right next to the portal of Gas Works Tunnel at the station throat. Another class A1 Pacific No 60156 Great Central has just reversed onto the turntable.

◀ The next few pictures feature a section of line Treacy really made his own. The stiff 1 in 107 gradient out of King's Cross called for just the sort of hard, uphill work from the engines he was after. It was in the stark, urban landscape between Gas Works and Copenhagen tunnels, somewhat ironically named Belle Isle, that he took some of his finest east coast main line shots. In this 1960 view, class A4 No 60003 Andrew K. McCosh ascends the bank, whilst class A3 No 60047 Donovan drifts downhill with an up express.

◀ *The whole railway environment is surely captured in this magnificent shot of Gresley class A3 4–6–2 No 60055* Woolwinder *storming up the bank out of King's Cross with the White Rose service for Leeds and Bradford. To the right a Thompson class A2/3 4–6–2 No 60524* Herringbone *awaits the road down to King's Cross station, having come off the shed.*

▲ *The sleek streamlined shape of class A4 No 60022* Mallard, *the world speed record holder for the steam locomotive, is shown off to advantage in this broadside portrait. The immaculately presented engine is coming off King's Cross depot, known as Top Shed, ready to reverse down the hill into the station to work the down* Elizabethan, *non-stop to Edinburgh.*

175

▲ A class N2 0–6–2T No 69492, fitted with condensing apparatus for working through the tunnels of the Metropolitan Widened lines to Moorgate, blasts up the hill towards Copenhagen tunnel. The locomotive is not heading for Hatfield, as the destination board indicates, but working a heavy empty stock train, including sleeping cars, out of King's Cross.

▶ King's Cross based class A3 Pacific No 60039 Sandwich passes under the North London line bridge, at Belle Isle, with the down 5.30pm departure, the Yorkshire Pullman, c 1961. It has recently been fitted with German style smoke deflectors to help lift the softer exhaust from the double chimney, which it received in 1959. Many of the LNER Pacifics were named after racehorses which had won classic races. Unfortunately some were not quite as euphonious as they might have been.

ENGINES
[MUS]T PASS
[WITHOUT
[ST]OPPING

60039

YORKSHIRE PULLMAN

GUARD

◀ *A step down from the Pacifics, the Gresley mixed traffic class V2 2–6–2s proved equally at home on fast freight or express passenger turns. No 60828 climbs Holloway bank with a down express in the summer of 1957. A Gresley articulated restaurant car set provides the train's catering facilities. Note the allotments on the embankment to the right, possibly a relic of the wartime Dig for Victory campaign.*

▶ *The morning sunshine flashes across the gleaming garter blue paintwork of No 4489* Dominion of Canada *as the streamlined Pacific charges through Finsbury Park with the down Flying Scotsman. The train is in the 1938/9 summer non-stop formation of 12 coaches. This means the corridor tender will be used, just north of York, to change crews. The bell was presented to the LNER by the Canadian Pacific Railway and fitted to No 4489 in 1938.*

179

LONDON – EUSTON

◄ *Journey's end. Two morning arrivals stand in platforms 1 and 2 of the old London Euston station. On the right Jubilee 4–6–0 No 45603* Solomon Islands *has brought in the overnight Irish Mail. In platform 2 rebuilt Patriot No 45514* Holyhead *brings its train to a halt.*

▲ *LMS class 4 2–6–4 tank No 2567 pulls a train of empty vans out of Euston under the Hampstead Road bridge c 1947. The high retaining walls of engineer's blue brick, laid in crisp English bond courses, are still a feature of the climb out of Euston.*

▲ *Crewe North (5A) allocated Princess Coronation No 46236* City of Bradford *pulls away from Euston with a down express for Holyhead c 1948. The engine took part in the locomotive exchanges of 1948. All 38 members of the class were recorded by Treacy in some 600 separate images. These covered virtually the whole period of its existence from 1937 to 1964.*

▶ *Princess Royal class 4–6–2 No 46210* Lady Patricia *ascends Camden bank with a northbound express c 1948. The old 'Premier Line' is still represented in this view as the leading coaches are of LNWR origin.*

▶ Three-cylinder Jubilee class
4–6–0 No 45733 Novelty *blasts
up Camden bank with the down
Midlander service for
Birmingham and
Wolverhampton c 1957. The
locomotive, based at
Wolverhampton Bushbury the
former LNWR shed, will have
worked the morning up service
from Wolverhampton and is
returning with the 5.50pm from
Euston.*

◀ *Another late afternoon
departure is headed by
unrebuilt Patriot class 4–6–0 No
45515* Caernarvon. *The Preston
based engine has just completed
the first mile out of Euston with
its northbound express. The
train is a relief working
probably for Blackpool.*

◀ Princess Coronation No 46239 City of Chester *passes its home depot, Camden, with the down Caledonian in 1957. It was the first year of operation for this Glasgow to Euston service which was limited to an eight-coach formation. The down train left Euston at 4.15pm.*

▲ *BR standard class 4 4–6–0 No 75030 passes Camden on the slow line with a seven-coach outer suburban service in the mid 1950s. It is returning to its home town of Bletchley with an evening semi fast train.*

▲ *Camden based Royal Scot No 6144 makes a fine sight as it hauls a northbound express past Kilburn in the late 1930s. It was running without a name at this time. The locomotive had previously carried the name* Ostrich *and in the mid 1940s was renamed* Honourable Artillery Company.

▶ *Blue streamliner No 6221* Queen Elizabeth *charges through Kilburn on a Saturday afternoon with the down Midday Scot for Glasgow, reporting number W97. In the late 1930s the Saturday service included the Coronation Scot set of coaches in its formation.*

LONDON – VICTORIA

Treacy did not get much opportunity to take photographs in the south. But when he was in London the exit from Victoria station was a favourite spot.

◄ *Bulleid brought many dramatic changes to the Southern as exemplified by Battle of Britain class Pacific No 21C157, later named* Biggin Hill. *It is seen here with the Golden Arrow on the 1 in 62 of Grosvenor bank climbing away from Victoria. The engine and train are fully clad in the Golden Arrow trimmings. The train was restored in April 1946 and this view was taken in 1947 when No 21C157 was only a few months old. The steam sanding gear was essential for a spirited attack on the bank not only because of the light axle weight but also the adverse effect of both curvature and flange lubricators.*

▶ *A pre-war boat train in the charge of Lord Nelson class 4–6–0 No 854* Howard of Effingham *makes an interesting comparison, taken a few yards nearer Victoria station, in the spring of 1939. The clock tower shows this is the 10.30am departure for Dover Marine. Stewarts Lane depot, Battersea, has provided an immaculate finish to No 854.*

CAMDEN

▲ *In the setting sun a group of Stanier locomotives turned to face north, coaled and watered await their next turn of duty at Camden shed in the 1950s. The atmosphere of the large locomotive shed has now gone for ever, but it still remains a* *vivid memory with those enthusiasts who waited their chance for a quick look when all seemed quiet. Treacy wonderfully captured the scene for posterity.*